D1200299

Listening to **Leaders**

Why Should I Listen to MY TEACHERS?

Christine Honders

PowerKiDS press™

NEW YORK

Published in 2020 by The Rosen Publishing Group, Inc.
29 East 21st Street, New York, NY 10010

Copyright © 2020 by The Rosen Publishing Group, Inc.

All rights reserved. No part of this book may be reproduced in any form without permission in writing from the publisher, except by a reviewer.

Editor: Greg Roza
Book Design: Rachel Rising

Photo Credits: Cover (insert), p. 17 wavebreakmedia/Shutterstock.com; Cover (background) Anna Nahabed/Shutterstock.com; pp. 5, 9, 11, 13, 15 Monkey Business Images/Shutterstock.com; p. 7 iofoto/Shutterstock.com; p. 19 antoniodiaz/Shutterstock.com; p. 21 stockfour/Shutterstock.com; p. 22 Ljupco Smokovski/Shutterstock.com.

Cataloging-in-Publication Data

Names: Honders, Christine.
Title: Why should I listen to my teachers? / Christine Honders.
Description: New York : PowerKids Press, 2020. | Series: Listening to leaders
Identifiers: ISBN 9781538341728 (pbk.) | ISBN 9781538341742 (library bound) | ISBN 9781538341735 (6 pack)
Subjects: LCSH: Teachers--Juvenile literature.
Classification: LCC LB1775.H66 2019 | DDC 371.1--dc23

Manufactured in the United States of America

CPSIA Compliance Information: Batch #CSPK19 For further information contact Rosen Publishing, New York, New York at 1-800-237-9932.

RICHMOND HILL PUBLIC LIBRARY
32972001666983 RV
Why should I listen to my teachers?
Nov.. 25, 2019

Contents

Ready to Learn

When you were born, your brain was ready to learn. After five years, you learned to walk, talk, and say your ABCs. Now your brain is ready for school! Teachers help us learn new things. It's important to listen to them so you'll do your best in school—and in life!

The Head of the Class

Teachers are the bosses of the classroom. They work hard to plan lessons every day. They come up with fun ways to learn new information. They make sure you're doing your work and help you if you don't understand something. Teachers want you to do your best.

Teacher Training

Teachers were students once, just like you. They went to college for special training so they know how to teach you. They also learn about kids and how their brains work. Teachers know what it's like to sit in a classroom and learn new things. That's why they're so good at helping you learn.

A Good Education

The teacher's main job is to help you get an **education**. They want you to get good grades so you'll be **successful**. They explain new things in a way that's easy to understand. Sometimes they take students on field trips. This helps kids understand that what they're learning is important in real life.

Getting to Know You

Teachers don't just give tests and homework. They watch you while you're working and playing. They want to know more about you. Teachers know that kids learn in many different ways. They see what you're good at and what you need help with. They figure out the best way to help each student do his or her best.

13

Teaching Is Caring

Most teachers love what they do. They wouldn't be working with kids if they didn't like them! It might not feel like it sometimes, but your teachers care about you. They're happy to teach you something new. They spend extra time with you because they don't want you to fail.

15

Teachers Outside the Classroom

Gym teachers make sure you get lots of exercise because healthy bodies help make healthy brains. Other teachers teach you new **skills**, like music or art. This helps kids learn different ways to **express** themselves. You might find that you're good at something that you've never even tried before!

A Student's Job

It's hard for teachers to do their jobs when students don't do their jobs. Teachers hand out homework and ask questions in class. This is so they can find out how much you've learned. But if you don't do your work, teachers won't know how to help you do your best.

Teachers Are People Too

It's **frustrating** when you don't understand something in class. You may get angry and want to stop listening to the teacher. Teachers work every day to help their students, and they want them to be on their best **behavior**. Teachers are people too, and giving them a hard time won't make your grades better.

Listening Is Learning

Good listeners are good learners. They **communicate** well with other people. They're better readers and writers. Good listening skills will help you get good grades and have a successful future. If you listen to your teacher now, you'll keep learning for the rest of your life.

Glossary

behavior: The way a person acts.

communicate: The use of words, sounds, signs, or behaviors to convey ideas, thoughts, and feelings.

education: The act of going to school and learning.

express: To make your feelings known.

frustrating: Making you feel that you can't get anything done.

skill: An ability that comes from training or practice.

successful: Reaching a goal or accomplishing what you planned to do.

Index

Websites

Due to the changing nature of Internet links, PowerKids Press has developed an online list of websites related to the subject of this book. This site is updated regularly. Please use this link to access the list: www.powerkidslinks.com/ltl/teachers